RAMA DRISHTI
INSIGHTS OF THE
AWAKENED SAGE

**DIRECT SEEING OF VERSES FROM
RAMA GITA - FIFTH CHAPTER OF
ADHYATMA RAMAYANA**

**NOT A COMMENTARY
NOT A TRANSLATION**

ISBN – 979-8-9897855-6-8

INTRODUCTION

Rama Drishti, is the DIRECT SEEING of the Vedantic instruction, The Rama Gita, given by Sri Rama to his younger brother Sri Lakshmana.

In this scripture, Rama encourages Lakshmana to directly see the truth that can be revealed only by intense self-inquiry and self-exploration.

This is neither a translation nor a commentary of the Rama Gita. Rather, every verse is a direct seeing, a revolutionary seeing. Seeing happens at the Witnessing level. You will have to excuse the intellect and set aside the mind. Attempt to see without the interference of memory.

The truths enumerated here may appear to be unknown in the beginning. An extended marination in the New Seeing may be in order.

Begin from the openness that emerges from the readiness to embrace the Unknown. Allowing the unknown to reveal your nature of the Beingness Beyond is an essential requirement.

Allow it to seep within and soon it will be revealed that it is not unknown because it is your Truth.

Be aware of the tremendous resistance from the identification of 'Being the person'. It will attempt to override your new Seeing of 'Being beyond'.

INTRODUCTION

You must allow the embedded belief of the 'person' to fade away and recognize that 'You are the Beyond'. You are that which is devoid of identification.

You were only fooled by the illusion of passion. You were only deceived by the imagination of pleasure. You were only ignorant about your true nature. This acknowledgment will take you far on this journey.

Merely believing my words will not get you there.
See it.
Embrace it.

NOTE:
This book is not a commentary on the verses. It is not even a direct translation. Commentaries and translations belong to the level of the intellect. This is not a novel. Consider it as a Sadhana. If you are new to the word, it will be explained on the next page.

This is a Direct Seeing of the Supreme Truth that lies beyond the intellect. The verse number indicates how that verse is directly seen by the Witnessing Awareness. Direct Seeing means seeing without the interference of memory [what is already known].

Go on! See!

THE SADHANA

Refrain from translating 'Sadhana' as a 'Practice'.
Sadhana is the complete Effacement of
conditioning. Effacement cannot be cultivated. It
is simply a natural release borne of 'Direct Seeing'.

So go on, See the truth while refraining from blind
belief.

THE SADHANA

Start with the recognition that, right in this
moment, you can recognize that you are the
witness of the eyes reading these words.

You abide beyond the body.

Take a moment to hold the stand of the beyond.

Do you recognize that you are beyond the mind
that is repeating these words?

Again, take a moment to hold the stand of the
beyond.

Then proceed forward...

Sri Rama Lived A Life Of Intense Penance.

Lakshmana Requested Rama Sincerely And
Earnestly, To Provide The Instruction On
Release From The Bondage Of Agnyana.
[Ignorance].

Lakshmana Had Purified Himself And Was
Earnest About His Spiritual Search.

Seeing His Longing For The Truth,
Sri Rama Began The Instruction of Gnyana
Yoga With A Description Of How One
Directly Sees The Truth.
[1-7]

The Body-Mind Person Appears.

Pleasant Sensation Manifests.

Attraction To Pleasantness Ensues.

Experiencership Is Assumed.

Story Of Doership Is Presumed.

Impressions Of Doership And Experiencership Are Threaded Together As Memory.

Memory Sprouts The Seeds Of Thought, Feeling, Sensation And Perception When Ready.

Sprouts Kick In The Belief Of Being The Body-Mind Person.

Body-Mind Person Reappears.
Rebirth Phenomena Recurs.
[8]

Ignoring The Fact Of One Arising At A
Time…

Being Unaware Of The Reality Of The
Background Of The NOW…

Oblivious To The Veracity Of Projection
Being Inside Out…

Negligent Of Its Respective Perception
Being Inside Out…

Nescient To The Actuality Of Being
Infinite Nobody-ness…

Are The Chief Causes Of The Rebirth
Phenomena Termed As Agnyana Or
Ignorance.

…*[Continued]*

Ignorance Births Personhood.

Personhood Begets Doership.

Doership Births Action.

Action Begets Experiencership.

Experiencership Births Impressions.

Impressions Beget Ignorance.

Action Cannot Exterminate Ignorance. It
Cannot Decimate What It Is Born Of.

Karma Yoga [Yoga Of Action] Cannot
Remove Agnyana [Ignorance].

Then What Can Annihilate Ignorance?

Nothing Other Than Knowledge Can
Replace The Lack Of Knowledge.

Only The Direct Seeing Of The Truth Can
Destroy Ignorant Blindness.

[9]

Lack Of Knowledge Assumes To Be The
Body.

Ignorance Assumes To Possess A Mind.

Nescience Assumes To Be An Individual
Entity.

Body-Mind-Person Is The Progeny Of
These Misidentifications.

Misidentification Begets Servility.

Servility To Thought.
Servility To Feeling.
Servility To Sensation.
Servility To Perception.

Action Born Of Servility Is But Evil.

Evil Action Is Fails To Avert The Endless
Loop Of Rebirth Phenomena.

Karma Yoga [Yoga Of Action] Cannot
Remove Agnyana [Ignorance]. Hence The
Insightful Seek Gnyana [Wisdom].
[10]

For Salvation, The Ritualists Argue That,

The Vedas Applaud Karma Yoga
[Path Of Action].

The Vedas Equally Praise Gnyana Yoga
[Path Of Wisdom].

The Vedas Commend That Both Paths
Complement Each Other.

Hence Karma Yoga Is Essential.
[11]

The Ritualists' Argument Continues:

The Vedas Proclaim That The Negligence
Of Prescribed Action Accrues Sin.

Hence The Spiritual Freedom Seeker Must
Always Indulge In Action.

Direct Seeing Refutes:
Gnyana Yoga Is Autonomously Efficient.
[12]

The Ritualists' Debate:

This Is The Untruth That Gnyana Is
Independent.

As Rituals Require Action,
Wisdom Must Require Action For Moksha.
[13]

Direct Seeing Asserts:

Once Personhood Is Assumed,
Doership Is Assumed.
Once Doership Is Assumed,
Doing Is Assumed.
Assumed Action Is But An Illusion.

The Illusion Of The Doing By The Doer Is
Guided By The Illusory Karma Yoga
Instruction Of Dropping Illusory
Expectations Of The Illusory Fruit Of The
Illusory Doing.

Action Is Hence An Illusion Born Of
Identification.
Wisdom Is The Reality Of The Canvas Of
The NOW On Which The Illusory Action
Wave Arises And Dissolves.

Hence Ego-Driven Illusory Action Cannot
Complement Ego-Devoid Wisdom Of The
Beyond.
Action Is Born Of False Identification
Wisdom Is Born Of Disidentification.
[14]

Karma Is The Arising.
Gnyana Is Its Backdrop.

Karma Is The Wave.
Gnyana Is The Water.

Karma Is The Dream World.
Gnyana Is The Deep Sleep Blankness.

Karma Is The Flame.
Gnyana Is What It Disappears Into.

Karma Is Born Of Ego-Sense [Ahamkaar
Vritti].
Gnyana Is Where The Ego-Sense Dies
[Vidyatma Vritti].

Illusory Karma Disappears Into The Reality
Of Gnyana Hence They Both Cannot Be
Lived Together.

The Illusory Person May Practice Illusory
Karma Yoga At First.
In Gnyana, Illusion Dissolves.
Then As A Siddha, Observe Illusory Karma
As A Happening.
[15]

Direct Seeing Urges:

Recognize The Un-Complementariness
Between Gnyana And Karma.

Honor The Truth Of The Flow That Elicits
Happenings Without Doership.

The Flow Triggers The Arising Of The
Sensation Of The Body.
That Is Assumed As The 'Person'.

The Flow Prompts The Arising Of The
Perception Of Sight, Sound, Smell, Taste,
Or Touch.
That Is Assumed As The 'World'.

The Flow Incites Doer-ship Connecting
The Person And The World.

Honoring The Flow, Graciously Renounce
The Assumptions Of:
- Being The Doer
- Doing An Action
- Being The Experiencer Of The World

Turn Inwards Towards The Backdrop Of
All These Illusory Arisings.

Turn Towards The Self!
[16]

Direct Seeing Urges:

On The Arising Of The Illusion Of
'I Am The Body',
Stay At A Distance And Witness.
Do Not Jump In.
Don't Assume To Be The Doer.

At The Witnessing Level, There Is An
Absence Of The Triggers Of Craving And
Aversion.

The Flow Itself Is The Spiritual Discipline
Of Selfless Action In The Absence Of
Craving And Aversion.
Karma Yoga Is A Natural Happening, Not
A Doing.

Know Your True Nature As The Witnessing
Awareness Space In Which The Arisings Of
Doership And Experiencership Arise And
Dissolve.

Abide In Your Nature Of Silence By
Renouncing The Noise Of Action.
[17]

Direct Seeing Urges:

Observe The I-Sense Arise.
Don't Get Fooled.
Don't Assume It To Be Real.
The 'I' Is Simply A Thought.
You Are Not A Thought.

Observe The I-Sense Dissolve.
Don't Get Fooled.
If You Were The 'I', Then Who Is It
Observing It Dissolve?
You Are Not That Which Disappeared.

When The Arising Of Action Emerges.
Don't Get Fooled.
Stay At A Distance And Observe The
Selfless Action Wave Dissolve.

When The Arising Of Experience Emerges.
Don't Get Fooled.
Stay At A Distance And Observe The
Impersonal Experience Wave Dissolve.

…*[Continued]*

Observing The Arisings,
Switch The Attention To The Equanimous
Background In Which They Dance.

Enfold Within.
Discern The Collapse Of The Witnessing
Awareness Into The Infinite Beingness.

Behold The Nature Of Your True Being As
An Alive Emptiness.
Dissolve! Repose! Abide!

Realize The Disappearance Of Maya.
Revere The Wisdom Of The Non-Duality
Of God, Self, And The World.
[18]

When The Nature Of The True Beingness
Is Recognized, All Duality And Diversity
Vanish.

'I' Vanishes.
'You' Vanishes.
'Mine' Vanishes.
'Yours' Vanishes.
'Doer' Vanishes.
'Experiencer' Vanishes.
'God' Vanishes.
'Devil' Vanishes.
'World' Vanishes.
Only The Flow Remains.

The Flow Does It All Without Doership Or
Experiencership.
Only The Flow Was.
Only The Flow Is.
Only The Flow Will Be.

Maaya's Spell Breaks.
Nothing Ever Happened.
Nothing Is Happening.
Nothing Will Ever Happen.

…[Continued]

Once You Have Seen It,
It Cannot Be Unseen.

Once You Have Realized It,
It Cannot Be Unrealized.

Once You Know The Magic Trick,
It Is Not Magic Anymore.

Once You Acknowledge The Illusory
Nature Of Maaya,
It Loses Its Grip On You.

Once Dead,
Maaya Is Not Born Again.
[19]

Once Maaya Is Rendered Powerless,
It Cannot Confuse The Witness Again.

The Conviction Of The 'Impossibility Of
Personhood' Anchors Itself Firmly.

The Conviction Of 'Non-Doership' Gains
A Tremendous Foothold.

The Conviction Of 'Non-Experiencership'
Becomes Strongly Entrenched.

Hence, What Can Germinate The Sprout
Of 'Karma Yogic' Understanding Of 'I Am
The Doer Of Selfless Action'?

How Can The Idea Of 'Acting Without
Anticipation' Ever Appear?

Hence Gnyana Yoga Can Independently
Lead One To Moksha.

Neither Karma Yoga Nor Any Other Yoga
Need Complement It.
[20]

Taittiriya Upanishad Advocates Renouncing
All Illusory Actions Including Those For
Heavenly Experiencership Pronounced By
Scriptures.

Brihadaaranyaka Upanishad Asserts That
Gnyana Is The Only Means. Karma Yoga's
Scope Is Way Too Limited For Moksha.

When Karma [Action] Is Limited To The
Waking State, How Can It Lead To Turiya
[The Fourth State]?

Without Stepping Beyond Turiya,
To Turiyatita [The Beyond],
Can There Be Moksha?

Karma Implies The Ego Of Doership.
Moksha Means Cessation Of The Ego.
How Can Karma Lead To Moksha?

Karma Is An Illusion. Moksha Is Reality.
How Can Illusion Deliver The Real?

[21]

Karma Is Dependent On The Illusion Of
Personhood.
Gnyana Is The Eradication Of The Illusion
Of Personhood.

Karma Is Dependent On The Illusion Of
Doership.
Gnyana Is The Effacement Of The Illusion
Of Doership.

Karma Is Dependent On The Illusion Of
Experiencership.
Gnyana Is The Elimination Of The Illusion
Of Experiencership.

Karma Is Dependent On The Illusion Of
The Existence Of A World.
Gnyana States That The World Is Unborn
[Ajaata].

Karma Is Dependent On An 'I' That Must
Do The Action.
Gnyana Emphasizes That There Is No
Individual Entity Only Universal
Consciousness.

The Declaration That Karma Complements
Gnyana Is Unjustified.
[22]

Oh! Personhood!
Immensely Vast Is Your Delusion.

Quit Persuading That 'I Am The Doer'.

Quit Convincing Me That 'I Am
Responsible'.

Quit Coaxing Me That 'I Will Sin If I Don't
Take Action'.

Quit Threatening Me That 'I Will
Experience The Effects Of Bad Karma.'

I Am The Witness Of The Person,
Not The Person.
I-The-Witness Cannot Act.
I-The-Witness Cannot Suffer Nor Enjoy.
I-The-Witness Hold No Responsibility.
I-The-Witness Bear Neither Sin Nor Virtue.

All Is The Grace Of The Flow.
Quit The Falsehood Of Ownership.
Renounce The Illusion Of Karma.
Abandon Desires To Change The Flow.
Honor! Respect! The Majestic Flow!
[23]

Oh! Maaya!
Your Spell Has Been Broken.
Your Charm Has Been Dispelled.
Your Enchantment Has Been Lifted.
Your Magnetism Has Faded.

I Am Bliss. I Am Beatitude.
I Am Unshakeable In The Conviction Of
The Absolute Truth.
I Am The Infinite Beingness.

I Am The Projectionist Of The Projections
Called God, Self, And The World.

All Is My Reflection.
All Is Me!
[24]

I Am That.
I-The-Witness Am Brahman.

I-The-Witness Had Forgotten My Identity.
I Searched For My Identity In Personhood.
I Searched For My Identity In The World.
I Eventually Found It Within.

I Have Recognized My True Self As None
Other Than The Infinite Beingness. I Am
That.

This Is What The Scriptures Proclaim, 'Tat
Tvam Asi'.
[25]

The Infinite Beingness Seemed Distant And Mysterious.

I Kept Seeking The Infinite Outside But Failed Again And Again.

The Futility Of Perceptions, Sensations, Thoughts, And Feelings, Soon Made Me Turn Away.

I-The-Witness Began Direct Self-inquiry.
Neti. Neti. Not This. Not This.
Negating The World.
Negating The Person.
I Arrived At The Witness And Hit A Glass Wall.
The Beingness Evaded Me, As If Playing Hide And Seek.

Until I Kept Seeking Within, I Couldn't Find It. When The Seeking Dissolved, The 'I-Sense' Collapsed.
The Drop Merged With The Ocean.
Beingness Revealed.

There Is No More An 'I' Yet All Is Me.
I Am Not, Yet I Am.
[26]

I Am Not, Yet I Am. I Am That Beingness.

Beingness Is Conscious Of The
'I-Sense' That Appears And Disappears In
It.

Beingness Does Not Claim To Be 'I'.

It Abides As The 'Not I' That Witnesses
The 'I-Sense'.

Beingness Is My Actual Identity.
Beingness Simply IS.
Beingness Is My True Nature.
I Am Not 'I'. I Am That.

That Is All There Is.
Ishvara Or God
Jiva Or Ego
Jagat Or World.

All Is Simply The Projected Desire Of
That.
Hence It Is All Maaya [Illusion].

Maaya First Projects The Dream World As
Subtle Thought Waves Of Ether, Air, Fire,
Water, And Earth.
[Panch Mahabhutas].
The Dream Projection Is Extended As The
Waking World. The Subtle Is Manifested As
The Gross.
Thus, The Illusion Of The World Is Born.

Simultaneously, Is Projected, The Dream
Subject That Is But Subtle Thought-Waves
Of Sound, Touch, Sight, Taste, And Smell.
[Panch Tanmatras].
The Dream Subject Projection Is Extended
As The Waking Subject.
The Subtle Is Manifested As The Gross
Thought.
Thus, The Illusion Of The Person Is Born.

…[Continued]

An Impression Of Desire Births A Subtle
Thought.
That In Turn Objectifies As A Gross
Thought.

In Actuality, The 'I' Is A Subtle Thought
Objectified As A Gross Manifestation.

In Reality, The World Is Merely A Subtle
Thought Objectified As A Gross
Manifestation.

Both The Perceiver And The Perceived Are
Mere Thought Waves.

…[Continued]

Birth Is A Thought Wave.

Karma Is A Thought Wave.

Pleasure Is A Thought Wave.

Pain Is A Thought Wave.

Death Is A Thought Wave.

Memory Puts These Thoughts Together
And Builds A Continuous Story Of
Consistent Personhood.

This Bundle Of Gross Thought Wave
Projections Is The Sthula Upadhi
[Being Is Disguised As The Gross Body].

In Actuality, There Is No Gross Physical
Body. It Is Simply Thought!
[28]

The Bundle Of Subtle Thought Wave
Projections Is The Sukshma Upadhi [Being
Disguised As The Subtle Body].

Mind Is A Subtle Thought Wave.

Intellect Is A Subtle Thought Wave.

Five Senses Of Perception Are Subtle
Thought Waves.

Five Organs Of Action Are Subtle Thought
Waves.

Five Pranas Are Subtle Thought Waves.

Five Tanmatras Are Subtle Thought Waves.

Joy Is A Subtle Thought Wave.

Sorrow Is A Subtle Thought Wave.

In Actuality, There Is No Subtle Body. It Is
Simply Thought!
[29]

The Absence Of The Waking Thought Is
Also A Thought.

The Absence Of Gross Thought Is Also A
Thought.

The Absence Of The Dream Thought Is
Also A Thought.

The Absence Of Subtle Thought Is Also A
Thought.

The Absence Of Arisings In Deep Sleep Is
An Absence-Thought.

…[Continued]

The Idea Of Absence Is Born Of The
Non-Apprehension Of Reality.

Non-Apprehension Is The Womb Of
Misapprehensions Of Reality That Are
Projected In The Dream And Waking As
Subtle And Gross Thoughts.

Memory Stores Impressions Of
Misapprehensions And Non-
Apprehensions.

The Three States Are Born Of These
Stored Impressions.

The Bundle Of Impression-Waves
Projection Is The Kaarana Upadhi.
[Being Disguised As The Causal Body].
[30]

The Projected Gross Physical Body [Annamayakosha] Echoes The Conscious Quality Of The Beingness.

The Projected Vital Airs [Praanamayakosha] Echo The Conscious Quality Of The Beingness.

The Projected Subtle Body Or Mind [Manomayakosha] Echoes The Conscious Quality Of The Beingness.

The Projected Subtle Intelligence [Vignyanamayakosha] Echoes The Conscious Quality Of The Beingness.

The Projected Absence [Anandamayakosha] Echoes The Blissful Quality Of The Beingness.

All Echoes Are The Progeny Of The Projecting Power Of Maaya.

…[Continued]

The Veiling Power Of Maaya Cannot
Obscure The Beingness For Long.

When The 'I' Collapses And Beingness Is
Revealed, Maaya Takes Off In A Dash.

The Beingness Appears To Be Enveloped
By These Sheaths [Koshas] But Remains
Ever Untainted.

The Beingness Appears To Be Mortal But
Remains Eternal.

The Beingness Appears To Come And Go
But Remains Ever-Immovable.

The Beingness Appears To Be Born
Repeatedly But Remains Ever-Unborn.

The Beingness Seems To Have Multiple
Sheaths But Ever-Remains One Without A
Second.
[31]

Projected Incomprehension Of Reality Is
Described As Tamas.

Tamas Veils The Truth.

The Veiling Notion Incapacitates The
Intellect.

Incapacitated Intellect In Turn Projects
Misapprehensions As Waking And Dream
Thoughts.

Projected Misapprehensions Are Described
As Rajas.

As The Witnessing Strengthens, Projected
Rajas And Tamas Are Recognized As Mere
Projections.

Not-Self. Not-Self.
Treating Them With Equal Vision
Illuminates The Sattva Of Turiya.

Turiya Leads Directly To The Absolute,
Eternal, All-Pervading Bliss Of The
Beingness.
[32]

The Projecting Power Of Incomprehension
Triggers The Illusions Of Body, Senses,
Prana, Mind, Intellect, And Their Absence,
Consecutively And Ceaselessly.

These Illusions Are Exhibited As Incessant
Thoughts Termed As Waking And
Dreaming.

The Ego-Sense Is Projected
To Dance To The Tunes Of The Thoughts.
Tossed Helplessly By Perpetual
Imaginations,
Ego Embeds Impressions Of Desires.

Tamas Bears Rajas.
Rajas Reinforces Tamas.
This Is The Cycle Of Samsara.
The Cycle Of Mere Illusions…

…[Continued]

Beingness Has No Body To Act.
There Is No Doer.

Beingness Has No Breath.
No One Breathes.

Beingness Has No Senses To Perceive.
There Is No Perceiver.

Beingness Has No Mind To Experience.
No One Feels Or Experiences.

Beingness Has No Mind To Think.
There Is No Thinker.

Beingness Has No Intellect To Analyze.
No One Intellectualizes.

There Is No Snake.
It Was Always A Rope.

[33]

When Awakened From The Illusion Of The
Snake,
The Wise Cannot Unsee The Seen.
He Cannot Hold On To The Snake That
Never Was.

When Awakened From The Illusion Of The
Body,
The Wise Cannot Unsee The Seen.
He Cannot Hold On To The Body That
Never Was.

When Awakened From The Illusion Of The
Breath,
The Wise Cannot Unsee The Seen.
He Cannot Hold On To The Breath That
Never Was.

When Awakened From The Illusion Of The
Mind,
The Wise Cannot Unsee The Seen.
He Cannot Hold On To The Mind That
Never Was.

When Awakened From The Illusion Of
The Intellect,
The Wise Cannot Unsee The Seen.
He Cannot Hold On To The Intellect That
Never Was.

…[Continued]

Decline The Tempting Suggestion From The First Arising Of Sensation Of The Body.

Refuse The Alluring Proposal Of The First Arising Of Thought.

Abandon The Seductive Lies Extended By The First Arising Of Feeling.

Snub The Enticing Offer Proffered By The First Arising Of Perception Of Sight.

Ignore The Attractive Fabrication Proposed By The First Arising Of Perception Of Sound.

Disallow The Inviting Notion Tendered By The First Arising Of Perception Of Smell.

Forsake The Captivating Illusion Cast By The First Arising Of Perception Of Taste.

Shun The Irresistible Appeal Delivered By The First Arising Of Perception Of Touch.

[34]

Direct Seeing Reveals:

The Beingness Has No Physical Body As
There Is No Matter.
The Beingness Has No Subtle Body As
There Is No Mind.
The Beingness Has No Causal Body As
There Is No Causality.

The Projections Of All Three Bodies, All
Three Gunas, All Five Koshas, And All
Three States Are Mere Illusions Of Maaya,
Like Colors In A Hologram.

The Idea Of Birth Is An Illusion.
The Idea Of Childhood Is An Illusion.
The Idea Of Adulthood Is An Illusion.
The Idea Of Seniority Is An Illusion.
The Idea Of Death Is An Illusion.

When The False 'I' Collapses Into The
Beingness,
It Relishes The Bliss;
It Savors Its Ancientness.
It Realizes Its Borderless Limitlessness;
It Recognizes How It Illuminates
Every Projection Of Its Hologram;
It Sees That It Is One Without A Second.
[35]

Direct Seeing Answers
Why Is There Sorrow In Blissful
Consciousness?

Because Reality Is Veiled,
The Seeking For It Generates Misery.
Because The World Illusion Is Made Of
Opposites,
The Ideas Of Sorrow And Joy Are Illusory.

Illusions Are Simply Misapprehensions
Born Of Non-apprehension Of Reality.
Illusions Are Rajas Born Of Tamas.
Illusions Are Ideas Of Names And Forms
Born Of
Namelessness And Formlessness.

Just Like The Snake Disappears When The
Rope Is Seen,
Both Sorrow And Joy Get Sucked Into The
Black Hole Of Equanimity On Awakening.

Lack Of Wisdom Is The Only Issue;
Wisdom Is The Only Solution.
[36]

Waves Of Illusory Perception Emerge From And Dissolve Into The Background Of The NOW.

Waves Of Illusory Thought Surface From And Vanish Into The Background Of The NOW.

Waves Of Illusory Feeling Come Forth From And Melt Away Into The Background Of The NOW.

Waves Of Illusory Sensation Arise From And Disperse Into The Background Of The NOW.

The Illusory Arisings Superimpose On The Reality Of The NOW.

The Illusory Snake Superimposes On The Reality Of The Rope.

Similarly, The Illusory Person And Its World Superimpose On The Beingness.

…[Continued]

The Blueness Of The Sky Is An Optical Illusion.
The Mirage In The Desert Is A Misjudgment.
The Ghost In The Post Is A Misperception.
Castles In The Air Is An Imagination.
These Are Entertained Because Of Misinterpretation.

Similarly, The Illusory Person Is A Misconception.
The Illusory World Is A Misbelief.
These Are Entertained Because Of The Non-Comprehension Of Reality.
[37]

Direct Seeing Of Reality Reveals How:

From The Formlessness Emerges The First
Subtle Form Of The Ego.
From Thoughtlessness Arises The First
Thought 'I'.

It Is The First Object That Surfaces From
The Objectlessness.
It Is The First Illusion To Manifest From
The Voidness Of Illusion.

It Is The Second To Emanate From The
One Without A Second.
It Is The First Creation Of Pain Borne Of
The Pain-Free All-Pervasiveness.

...*[Continued]*

The 'I' Births 'I Am The Person'.
'I Am The Person' Births
'I Am The Doer', 'I Am The Thinker', And
'I Am The Feeler'.
That In Turn Births
'I Am The Experiencer'.

All This Constitutes The Imagined
Conceptual, Individualized Self.
In Reality, There Is No Individual Soul,
There Is No 'I'. Only Beingness Is!

Just As A Cobra Is Untouched By The
Lethality Of Its Own Venom;
So, The Emptiness Of The Beingness Is
Ever Unoccupied And Free Of The
Projections Of Maaya.
[38]

Pleasant Sensation Waves Appear And
Disappear.
Unpleasant Sensation Waves Appear And
Disappear.
Good Thought Waves Appear And
Disappear.
Bad Thought Waves Appear And Disappear.
Craving Feeling Waves Appear And
Disappear.
Aversion Feeling Waves Appear And
Disappear.

Perception Of Sight Waves Appear And
Disappear.
Perception Of Sound Waves Appear And
Disappear.
Perception Of Smell Waves Appear And
Disappear.
Perception Of Taste Waves Appear And
Disappear.
Perception Of Touch Waves Appear And
Disappear.

That Is Samsara!

…[Continued]

Samsaric Waves Have An Illusory
Synchrony
Limited To Waking And Dreaming But
Absent In Deep Sleep.

The 'I-Sense' Too Is Present In Waking And
Dreaming
But Absent In Deep Sleep.

When The 'I-Sense' Is, Perceptions,
Sensations, Thoughts, And Feelings Are.

When The 'I-Sense' Is Not, Perceptions,
Sensations, Thoughts, And Feelings Are
Not.

Samsara Belongs To The 'I-Sense'.
Illusion Happens To Illusion.

The Reality Of Beingness Remains Ever
Untouched;
As Is Directly Seen By Being The Witness
Of The Three States [Turiya].
[39]

Beingness Radiates Its Inherent Quality Of
Consciousness To The 'I-sense' Like The
Sun That Innately Shines.

The Borrowed Consciousness Of The 'I'
Further Reflects And Identifies With A
Thought Wave And Assumes To Be A
Conscious Mind.

The Borrowed Consciousness Of The
'Mind' Further Reflects And Identifies With
A Sensation Wave;
Thus, It Assumes To Be A Conscious Body.

The Borrowed Consciousness Of The
'Body' Further Reflects And Identifies With
Perception Waves Of Sight, Sound, Smell,
Taste, And Touch;
Thus, It Assumes To Experience An
Independently Existing World.

…[Continued]

Neither The Body, Nor The Mind, Nor The
World Is Conscious By Itself;
Their Appearance Of Being Conscious Is A
Temporarily Borrowed Power Limited To
Waking And Dreaming.

These Reflections Rest In The Deep Sleep
As If Run Out Of Their Borrowed Power.
When Charged Again, These Reflections
Reappear And That Is Termed As The
Waking And The Dream.

The Projecting Power Of Maaya Plays The
Game Of Reflections.
All Illusions Belong To The Beingness
Yet It Remains Ever Unaffected By Its
Magic Show.
[40]

The Sun In The Sky Reflects In The Still
Water Of The Lake Giving The False
Appearance Of The Sun-in-the-lake;
So Is The Reflected Consciousness
[Chittachaaya] Of The Beingness.

When The Sun In The Lake Dances,
The Sun In The Sky Remains Unaffected.
When Thoughts, Feelings, Sensations, And
Perceptions Consume The 'I-sense', The
Beingness Remains Unaffected.

When An Iron Ball Is Brought In Proximity
To The Fire, The Redness And Heat Are
Projected Onto It.
Similarly, The Conscious Quality Is
Reflected In Imagined Arisings.

The Product Of This Superimposition Is
An Existence [World],
Consisting A Conscious Personality,
With A Conscious Mind And Intellect.
[41]

When The Wave Of Earnestness In The Seeker Peaks.
Listening Sincerely To The Words Of The Enlightened Peaks.
Contemplation, Inquiry, And Inner Explorations Peak.
Then Only The Inner Guru Shines His Light.
Direct Seeing Reveals The Truth Of The Samsara-Magic-Trick.
Inward Turning Happens Due To The Futility Of The Magic.
Beingness Is Revealed By The Collapse Of The 'I-Sense'.

Brahman Satyam [Only Brahman Is] Is Realized.
The Next Automatic Realization Is Jagat Mithya [World Is An Illusion].

Then The Illusory Person In An Illusory World Is No Longer Alluring.
The Magic Dissipates.
The Spell Shatters.
The Enchantment Fades Away.
[42]

From The Vantage Point Of The Beingness,
The 'I-Sense', The Mind, The Intellect, The
Body, The Senses, The Prana, The World
Of Events, Objects, And Personalities,
All Are Seen Simply Like Light Effects Of
The Hologram Of Consciousness.

Its Light Is Unborn And Undying.
There Is Only Light And No Second.
Its Light Is Ever-resplendent.

The Light Is Ever Pure And Untainted By
The Mass Of Perceptions, Sensations,
Thoughts, Feelings, Or Their Absence.

The Hologram Is Infinite; Beginningless
And Endless.
All Happens In It, Yet It Is Actionless And
Experienceless.

I Am The Light. I Am The Hologram.
I Am The Consciousness.
I Am The World.
I Am Holiness And Bliss Itself.
[43]

Direct Seeing Reveals:

I-The-Hologram Of Consciousness, Am
Eternally Free Of The Waking, Dream, And
Sleep Light Effects Of Perception,
Sensation, Thought, Feeling, The 'I' Or
Their Absence Dancing Within Me.

I-The-Hologram Of Consciousness, Hold
Indescribable Powers Of Projection Of The
Hologram And The Veiling Of My Nature
Of Light.

I-The-Hologram Of Consciousness, Cannot
Be Comprehended By The Individual Light
Effects Like The Mind And Intellect.

...[Continued]

Direct Seeing Reveals:

I-The-Hologram Of Consciousness,
Am Unchangeable Despite The Changing
Perceptions, Sensations, Thoughts, Feelings,
And The 'I-Sense' Within Me.

I-The-Hologram Of Consciousness,
Neither Have A Border, Nor A Limit,
Nor An End.

Only I AM, Nothing Else Is.
Basking In The Glory Of My Truth,
I Abide Blissfully.
[44]

But The 'I-sense' Has A Short Memory And
Easily Gets Consumed.
Perceptions, Sensations, Thoughts, And
Feelings, Constantly Entice It.

Hence Repeated Immersion In The Pure
Witnessing Destroys Ignorance By
Revealing The Beingness.
Like Regular Medicine Finally Treats The
Disease.

Holding On To The Stand Of The Witness
Is Key.
Rejecting The Temptations Of Personhood,
Doership, And Experiencership Is Essential.
Intensely Longing For Beingness Is Crucial.
One-Pointedness For Beingness Is
Paramount.
[45]

Direct Seeing Insists:

One Glimpse Of The Beingness Is
Insufficient Oh Dear 'I-Sense'.
Halt Your Dance, Take A Breath.
Step Back And Simply Witness.

Witness The Perception Of Sight Arise And
Fall. Don't Jump In. Stay. Abide.

Witness The Perception Of Sound Arise
And Fall. Don't Jump In. Stay. Abide.

Witness The Perception Of Smell Arise
And Fall. Don't Jump In. Stay. Abide.

Witness The Perception Of Taste Arise And
Fall. Don't Jump In. Stay. Abide.

Witness The Perception Of Touch Arise
And Fall. Don't Jump In. Stay. Abide.

...*[Continued]*

Direct Seeing Continues:

Witness The Thoughts Arise And Fall.
Don't Jump In. Stay. Abide.

Witness The Feelings Of Sound Arise And
Fall. Don't Jump In. Stay. Abide.

Witness The Sensations Arise And Fall.
Don't Jump In. Stay. Abide.

Motionlessly Watch.
Unmovingly Observe.
Fixedly Gaze.
View In Stillness.
Unflinchingly Witness.

Abide Until
The Observer Dissolves,
The Watcher Disappears,
The Gazer Fades Away,
The Viewer Dissipates,
The Witness Collapses,
Only The Light Of Beingness Remains…
[46]

Direct Seeing Continues:

Whenever The Light Disappears And You
Find Yourself Assuming Personhood Again,
Step Back And Witness.

An Arising Of Magnificent Power Arises,
Peaks And Troughs,
Stay, Don't Slip,
Observe It Until It Dissolves,
Now Question What It Dissolves Into.

That Is The Gap Between Arisings.
That Is The Backdrop Of The Now.
That Is The Naked 'I'
Without This Or That.
That Is The Invisible Light Of
Consciousness.

Hold On To The Lifeline Of The Light.
Merge. Dissolve. Disappear.
No Outer. No Inner. No Name. No Form.
Simply A Limitless Source Of Bliss.
[47]

Direct Seeing Hints:

If You Keep Slipping From Your
Witnessing Stand,
Attempt An In-Between Stepping Stone,
Recognize The Vibration Of Creation,
The Anhad Naad [Limitless Tune],
The Substance Of All Names And Forms.

When The Arising Of Name And Form
Grips You,
Attempt To Recognize The Anhad Naad
That It Is Made Of,
Shift The Attention From The Arisings To
The Naad Or Aum.
Merge. Dissolve. Disappear.

Notice That The Duality Disappears.
Notice The Naad Disappear.
No Outer. No Inner. No Name. No Form.
Simply A Limitless Source Of Bliss.
[48]

Direct Seeing Hints At Utilizing Aum As A
Stepping Stone To Samadhi.

Aum Is Amplified In The Waking Names
And Forms.
Hence The Syllable 'Aaa' Represents The
Waking.

Aum Is Softer In The Dream Names And
Forms,
Hence The Syllable 'Uuu' Represents
Dreaming.

Aum Is Imperceptible In The Sleep
Absence Of Names And Forms,
Hence, The Syllable 'Mmm' Represents
Sleeping.

Using The Syllables, One Transcends The
Waker, Dreamer, And Sleeper;
The Transcendental Silence Of The NOW
Is Attained,
That Is Turiya [The Fourth].
Turiyatita [The Transcendence],
Lies Beyond.
[49]

Recognize In Your Swapna Nidra Gnyana
Sadhana That The Waking Perceptions,
Sensations, Thoughts, And Feelings
Automatically Merge Into The Dream.
The Dream Perceptions, Sensations,
Thoughts, And Feelings Automatically
Merge Into The Deep Sleep.

Similarly, Using AUM As A Guide For
Nirvikalpa Samadhi,
Witness The Disappearance Of The Naad
Along With The Waking Perceptions,
Sensations, Thoughts, And Feelings.

Witness, The Naad Becoming Softer With
Fuzzy Perceptions, Sensations, Thoughts,
And Feelings,
Recognize Them Automatically Merging
Into The Nothingness Of The NOW As If
Dissolving In Sleep.

…*[Continued]*

Simply Witnessing The Naad Is The Key To
Samadhi,
Witness Without Imagination,
Observe Without The Interference Of
Memory,
As All That Is Name And Form.

AUM Is A Vibration,
Actually, Nameless And Formless,
Agree To Be Without The Crutches Of
Name And Form.
Simply BE!

Reject All Perceptions, Sensations, Feelings,
And Thoughts.
Be With The Vibration Of The Universe
Without Using The Word 'AUM'.
Simply BE!
[50]

Aaa Dissolves Into Uuu.
Uuu Dissolves Into Mmm.
Mmm Vanishes.

Waker-I And Its Waking World Enfold Into
The Dreamer-I And Its Dreamworld, Which
In Turn,
Merge Into The Deep Sleep Darkness. Even
The Sleeper-I Resolves.

The Gross And The Subtle Merge Into The
Causal Principle Of Ishvara [God], Which
In Turn Unites With The Brahman.

The Presence As Well As The Absence Of
Names And Forms Vanishes
Leaving Behind The Non-Dual Higher
Witnessing Space.

…[Continued]

The 'I-sense' Notices The Void.
Due To Old Habits, It Seeks And Seeks.
When It Finds Nothing, Seeking Halts.
Respite Ensues.

Namelessness And Formlessness Are
Accepted.

Freedom From The Binding Fetters Of
Perception, Sensation, Thought, And
Feeling Is Acknowledged.

The Sweet Bliss Of The Equanimity Of
Emptiness Is Savored.

Non-Duality Is Tasted.

The Eternal Light Of The Void Is
Perceived.

The Truth, 'I Am The Supreme Brahman' Is
Realized.
[51]

There Is The Recognition That I Am That
Light Of Consciousness Which Is
Projecting A Picture Or Hologram Of A
Person In A World.

There Is The Realization That The Person
Picture And The World Picture Are Made
Of Me-The-Consciousness.

There Is The Acknowledgment Of The
Absence Of An Independently Existing
World Made Of Matter.

There Is Concurrence With The Truth Of
Non-Doership And Non-Experiencership.

…[Continued]

Direct Seeing Reveals The Oneness Of:

Seer, Seeing, Seen.

Hearer, Hearing, Heard.

Toucher, Touching, Touched.

Smeller, Smelling, Smelled.

Taster, Tasting, Tasted.

Thinker, Thinking, Thought.

Feeler, Feeling, Felt.

Sensor, Sensing, Sensation.

Beingness, Witness, Person And World.

Agnyana [Non-Apprehension] And Dvaita
Pratiti [Misapprehensions] Evaporate.
Tranquil Emancipation Transpires Leaving
Behind Divine Bliss.
[52]

Sensation Of Hunger Surfaces And
Retreats.
Perception Of Sight Of Food
Appears And Fades Away.

Perception Of Action Of Eating
Materializes.
Sensation Of Taste Emerges And
Dissipates.
Sensation Of Fullness Arises And
Dissolves.
Perception Of Action Of Eating
Dissolves.

The Flow Simply Manifests One
Arising After Another.
'I -Sense' Witnesses The Perceptions
And Sensations Without Grasping.

Perception Of Action Of Eating Is
Halted.

Not Craving For Anything From The
Body Is Samadhi.

…[Continued]

Feelings Of Unhappiness Surface And
Retreat.
Perception Of Sight Of Painful Object
Appears And Fades Away.

Memory Thought Of A Similar Event
Related To The Object Emerges And
Dissipates.
Feelings Of Unhappiness Related To The
Memory Arise And Dissolve.

The Flow Simply Manifests One Arising
After Another.
'I-sense' Witnesses The Perceptions And
Feelings Without Grasping.

Perceptions, Thoughts, And Feelings Pass
Away.

Not Detesting Anything Of The Mind Is
Samadhi.

…[Continued]

Feelings Of Passion Surface And Retreat.
Perception Of Sight Of Pleasant Object
Appears And Fades Away.

Memory Thought Of A Similar Event
Related To The Object Emerges And
Dissipates.
Feelings Of Passion Related To The
Memory Arise And Dissolve.

The Flow Simply Manifests One Arising
After Another.
'I-Sense' Witnesses The Perceptions And
Feelings Without Grasping.

Perceptions, Thoughts, And Feelings Pass
Away.

Not Craving For Anything From The Mind
Is Samadhi.

...*[Continued]*

Thoughts Of Aging And Death Surface
And Retreat.
Perception Of The Body Appears And
Fades Away.

Perception Of Action Of Retirement And
Will-Planning Materializes.
Feelings Of Fear Of Death Emerge And
Dissipate.
Memory Thoughts Related To Aging And
Death Arise And Dissolve.
Perception Of Action Of Retirement And
Will-planning Dissolves.

The Flow Simply Manifests One Arising
After Another.
'I-Sense' Witnesses The Perceptions,
Thoughts, And Feelings Without Grasping.

Not Lusting For Anything From The Body-
Mind Is Samadhi.

...*[Continued]*

Kama [Lust], Krodha [Anger],
Lobha [Greed], Moha [Delusion],
Mad [Arrogance], Matsar [Jealousy] Surface
And Retreat.
Perception Of Sight Of Related Object
Appears And Fades Away.

Memory Thought Of A Similar Event
Related To The Object Emerges And
Dissipates.
Feelings Related To The Memory Arise
And Dissolve.

The Flow Simply Manifests One Arising
After Another.
'I-Sense' Witnesses The Perceptions And
Feelings Without Grasping.

Perceptions, Thoughts, And Feelings Pass
Away.

Not Grasping Nor Resisting Anything Of
The Mind Is Samadhi.
[53]

Surrendering To The Flow Is Felicity.

Renouncing The False Doer-ship Is
Beatitude.

Relinquishing False Experiencership Is
Blessedness.

Ceding Ownership Of Perceptions,
Sensations, Thoughts, And Feelings Is
Serenity.

Constantly Honoring The Flow And
Revering Its Magnitude Is Euphoria.

Being Vulnerable To The Beingness,
Allowing The 'I' To Dissolve Into It,
Is Nirvana.

This Samadhi Eventually Melts Away The
Wax-like Ego.
Union With The Supreme Ensues.
[54]

Samadhi Is:

Renouncing All Prescribed Sadhanas For
The Body,
Rejecting All Suggested Sadhanas For The
Mind,
Declining To Limit Oneself To The Wakers'
Body-Mind.
Refusing To Think Of Oneself As A
Person,
Recognizing Everything Including The 'I'
As Momentary And Hence Fearsome.

Free From Religious, Social, And Cultural
Conditionings,
One Who Honors The Flow,
Maintains The Witnessing Stand,
Without Compromising On His Reality,
Attains Oneness [Non-Duality] With All.
[55]

The 'I-Sense' Remains As The Pure
Witnessing Space:

Recognizing The Oneness With
Perceptions, Sensations, Thoughts, And
Feelings.

Recognizing That There Is Simply A
Dimensionless Awareness,
And No Individual Entity.

Seeing Directly The Timeless Center Of
Observation, Devoid Of An Observer,
Devoid Of The Observed.

Seeing The Pure Light Of The Beingness.

The 'I' Finally Merges Into The Light, And
All Name-Form Projections Of Earth,
Water, Fire, Air, And Ether Dissolve Too.

The Drop Merges Into The Ocean To
Never Return.
[56]

Perception Of Ignorant People Drowned In
Illusion,
Arise And Fall.

Undeluded By The Illusion Of The
Ceaseless Perceptions,

Realizing That Perceptions Are Reflections
Of Past Projections Of Desires,

Knowing That Prarabdha Will Manifest
Until Exhaustion,

Accepting The Current Of The Flow,
Harmonizing With The Natural Rhythm,

Rejecting Names And Forms As Illusory,

Non-Compromising With The Reality Of
Brahman,

All Confusions Rest.
[57]

Constantly Immersed In Pure Witnessing,
Knowing That The Work Is Not Done
Until Jagat Mithya [The World Is An
Illusion] Is Completely Unveiled.

Earnest, Authentic,
Intense, And Resolute,
Incessantly Abide,
Devoid Of Over-Confidence,

Only To The Longing Heart,
Is Revealed The Glory Of The Beingness,
From Saguna To Nirguna,
From Witnessing To Being.

Revel In The Dimensionless
Until A Point Of No Return Arrives When
The Merged Drop Cannot Be Separated
From The Ocean.

Until Then The Work Is Not Done.
[58]

The Wave Of The Secret Has Arisen And Dissolved.

All That Could Be Revealed Has Been Enumerated.

Follow The Truths And Attempt To See Them Directly.

Die Before Death. Let The Person Die. Let The World Come To Dissolution.

Liberate Yourself From All Fetters Of Ignorance.

See What I See!
[59]

Allow The NOW To Erase All Illusions,
Be At Ease With The Emptiness Of The
NOW.

Renounce Identification.
Reject Delusion.

Be Blissful!
Bask In The Beatitude Of The Supreme
Being!
[60]

Be Devoted To The Formlessness!
You Will Soon Lose All Form.
Just Like A Drop Merges With The Ocean.
Just Like Sunlight Devours All Darkness.

This Tip Is Sufficient For Self-Realization.
For Anyone Earnest Enough To Follow
This.

Holiness Will Follow If You Follow
Formlessness.
Love Will Follow If You Follow The Truth.
[61]

One Who Is Devotedly Surrendered To The
Beingness Compels Its Divine Unification.
[62]

The Beginning!

ABOUT THE AUTHOR

Wisdom Is Universal And Eternal. It Cannot Be
Created, Manufactured, Produced, Or Destroyed. It
Cannot Be Owned Or Possessed. It Is Never Personal.

Every Wave Possessing The Yearning To Know Itself
Can Find The Ocean. On Discovering The Ocean, It
Cannot Claim Ownership Of The Ocean. It Is Not.

The Spiritual Wisdom Belongs To Nobody.
Nobody-ness Is The Author. Nothingness Is The
Source.

Ekta Bathija Is Merely The Medium Through Which
Nothingness Channelized The Swapna Nidra Gnyana
Sadhana Wisdom Into Words. Do Not Get Attached To
The Medium. Go Directly To The Source.

May The Nothingness Help Reveal The Supreme Truth
Of What You Truly Are!

Website: https://ektabathija.com/
Email: AncientWisdomPearls@gmail.com
Gnyana Sangha Inc. USA

OTHER BOOKS BY THE AUTHOR

Spiraling Avenues: Waking, Dreaming, Sleeping, Being: Swapna Nidra Gnyana Sadhana Volume I

Beyond The Veil Of Dream And Sleep: Swapna Nidra Gnyana Sadhana - Volume II

Black Hole Of Equanimity: Rama Drishti: Direct Seeing Of Rama Gita.

Insight Of Dispassion: Vairagya Drishti: Direct Seeing Of Vairagya Shatakam.

365 Insights That Liberate: Advaita Drishti: Volume 1: Direct Seeing Of Non-Duality

It's A Rope Not A Snake: Adhyaasa Drishti: Volume 1: Direct Seeing Of Adhyaasa Bhashya

I: Ko'Ham Drishti: Direct Seeing Of Who Am I [Nan Yar]

Be Spiritually Independent Because There Is No External Guru: Guru Tattva Drishti

Viveka Journal Level I

Viveka Journal Level II

OTHER BOOKS BY THE AUTHOR

Buddha Journal Level I

Buddha Journal Level II

Buddha Journal Level III

Buddha Journal On The First Jhana

Buddha Journal On The Second Jhana

Buddha Journal On The Third Jhana

Buddha Journal On The Fourth Jhana

Buddha Journal On The Base Of Infinite Space

Buddha Journal On The Base Of Infinite Consciousness

Buddha Journal On The Base Of Nothingness

Buddha Journal On The Base Of Neither Perception Nor Non-perception

Buddha Journal On Cessation Of Perception And Feeling

www.ingramcontent.com/pod-product-compliance
Lightning Source LLC
Chambersburg PA
CBHW060345050426
42449CB00011B/2841